1 PIANO, 4 HANDS

PIANO DUET PLAY-ALONG

VOLUME 39

LENNON & McCARTNEY HITS

To access audio, visit:
www.halleonard.com/mylibrary

7348-6982-0371-6560

ISBN 978-1-4234-8043-3

7777 W. Bluemound Rd. P.O. Box 13819 Milwaukee, WI 53213

Visit Hal Leonard Online at
www.halleonard.com

CONTENTS

ALL YOU NEED IS LOVE

SECONDO

Words and Music by JOHN LENNON
and PAUL McCARTNEY

ALL YOU NEED IS LOVE

PRIMO

Words and Music by JOHN LENNON
and PAUL McCARTNEY

Moderately, like a march

20
3
3

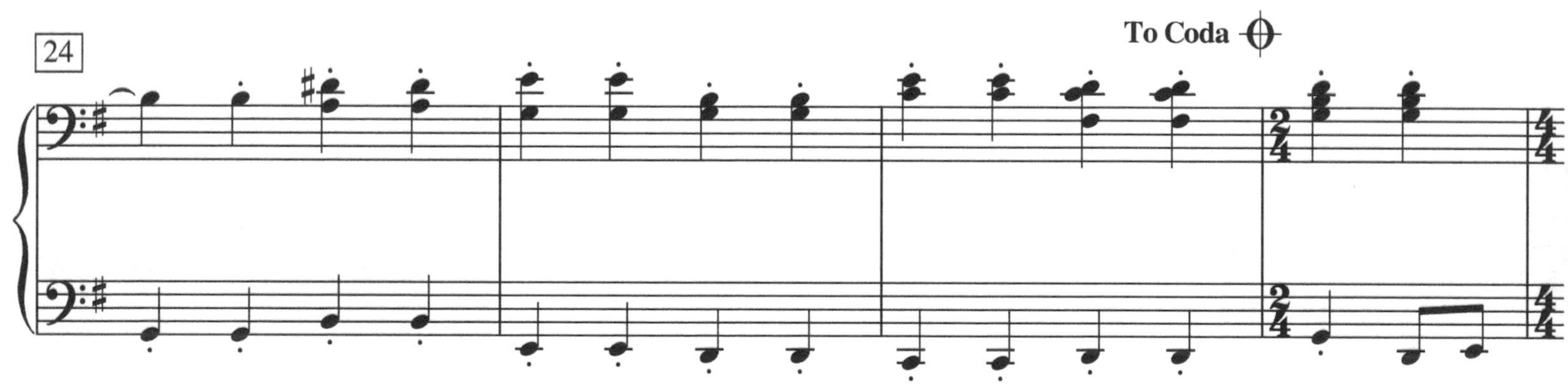
24
To Coda

28
mp

33
f
3

20
3
2
1
3
2
1

24
To Coda
4
3

28
mf

33
tr
f
3
2
1

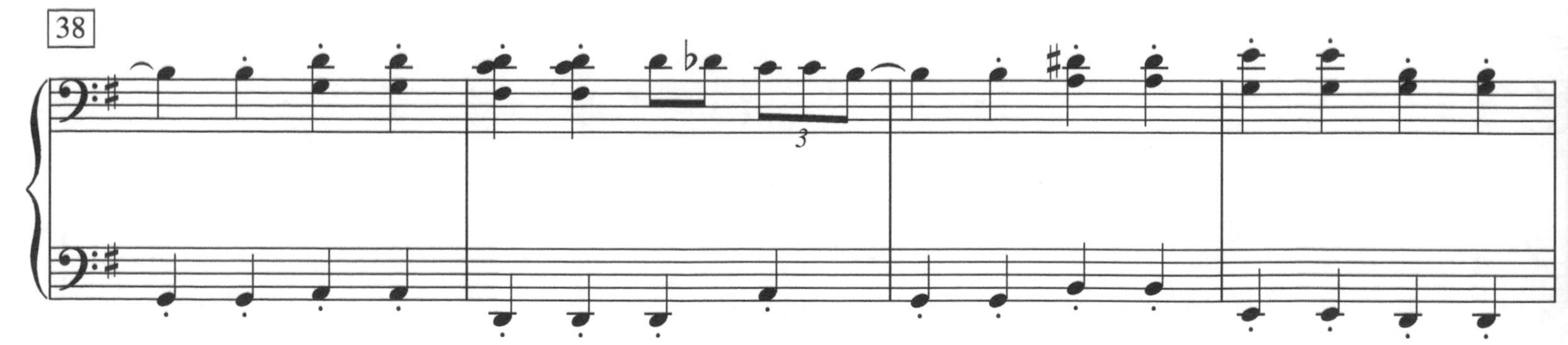
38
3

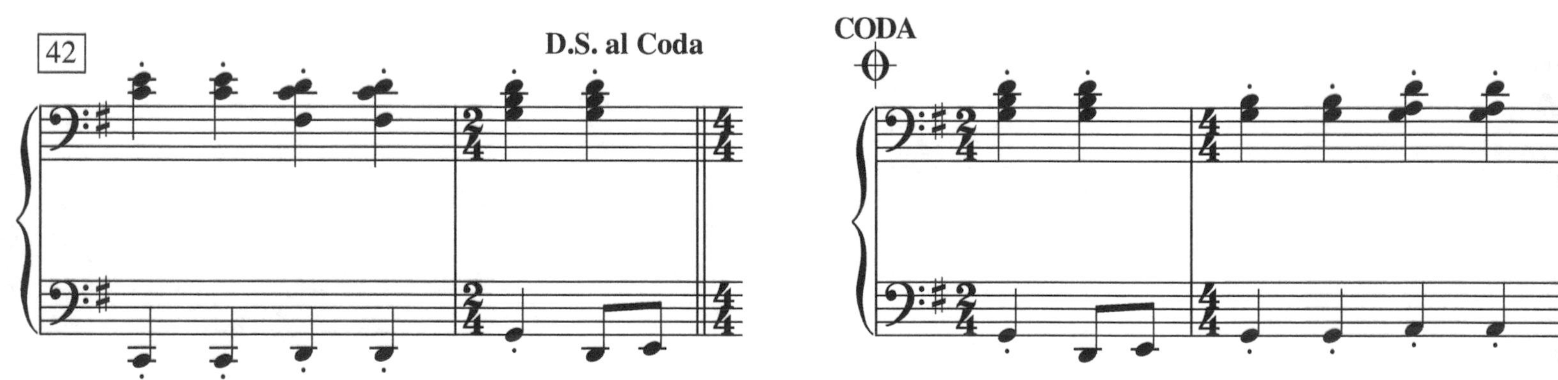
42
D.S. al Coda
CODA

46
3
3

50

PRIMO

BLACKBIRD

SECONDO

Words and Music by JOHN LENNON
and PAUL McCARTNEY

BLACKBIRD

PRIMO

Words and Music by JOHN LENNON
and PAUL McCARTNEY

17
f
mp

21
p
cresc.

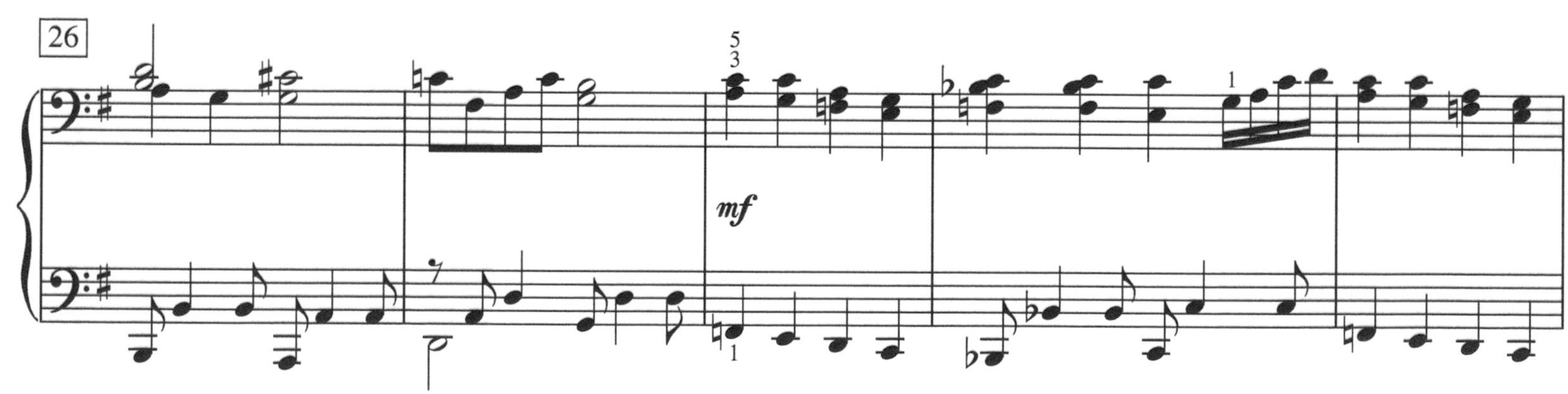
26
mf

31
f
mp

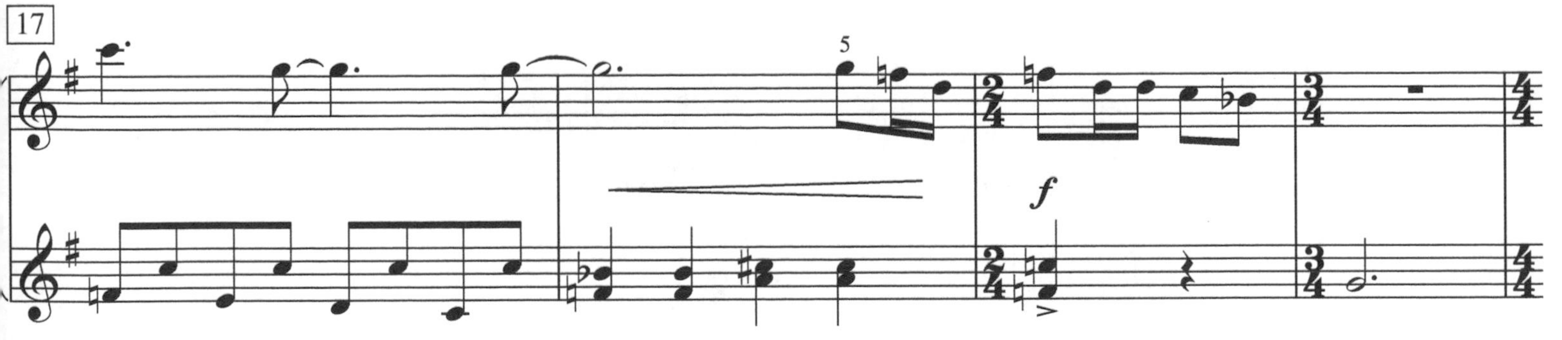
17
5
f

21
mp
cresc.

26
5
f

31
5
f
mp

SECONDO

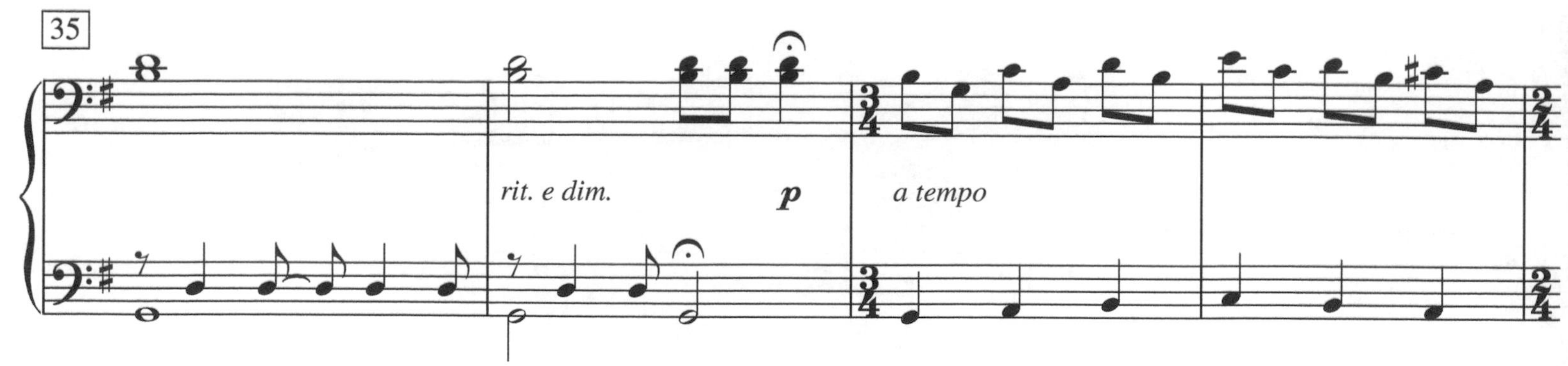

PRIMO

DAY TRIPPER

SECONDO

Words and Music by JOHN LENNON
and PAUL McCARTNEY

Moderate Rock

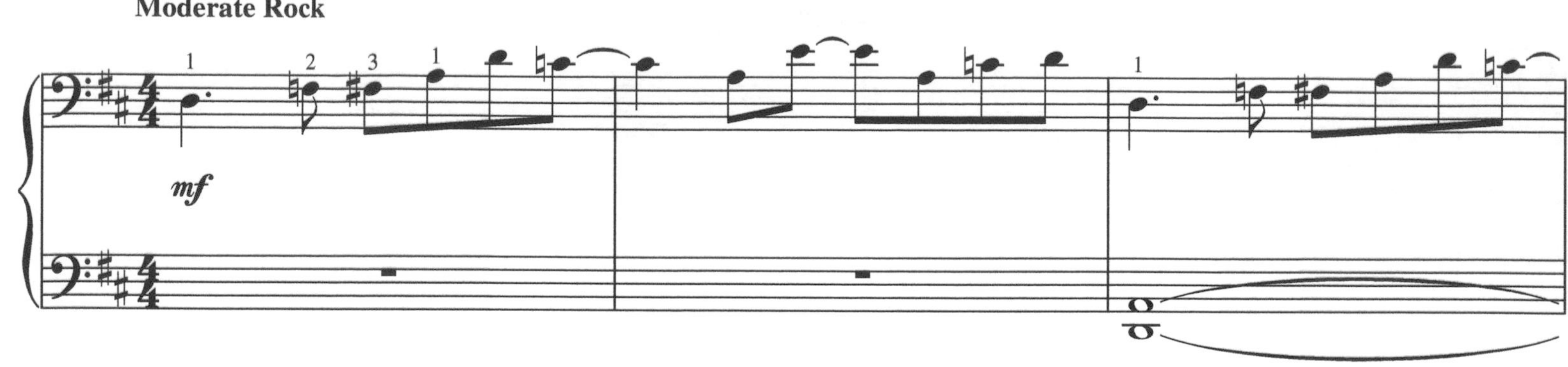

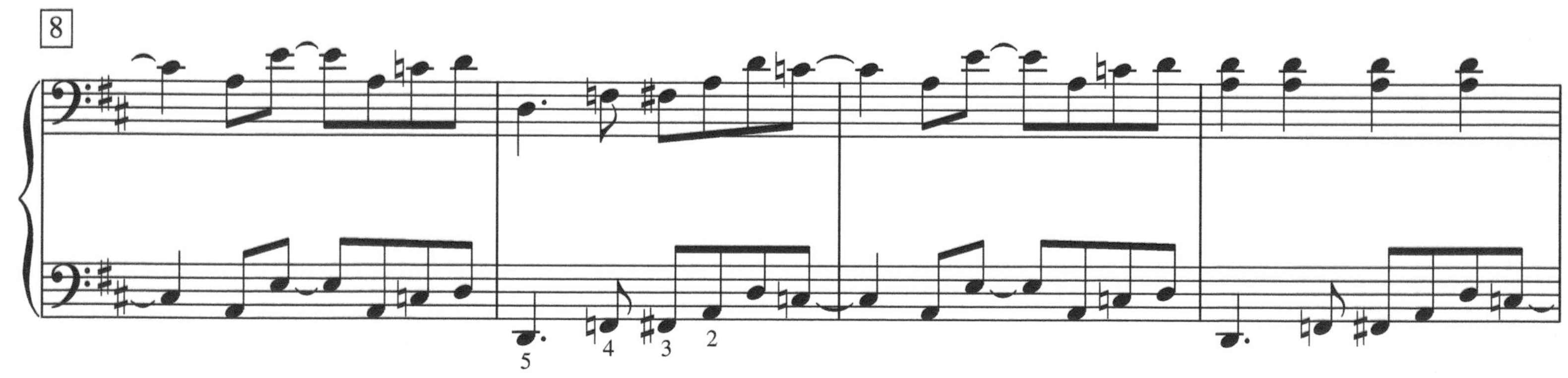

DAY TRIPPER

PRIMO

Words and Music by JOHN LENNON
and PAUL McCARTNEY

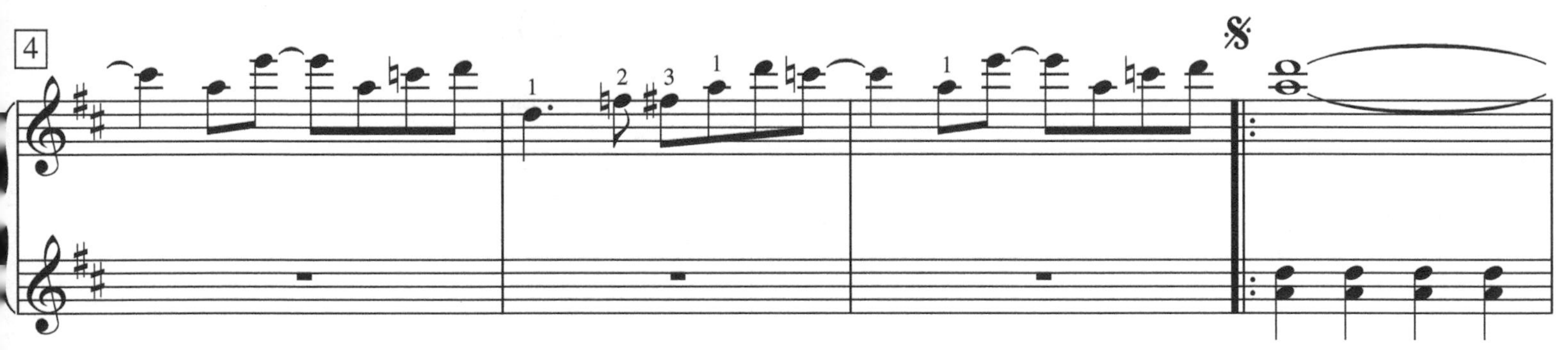

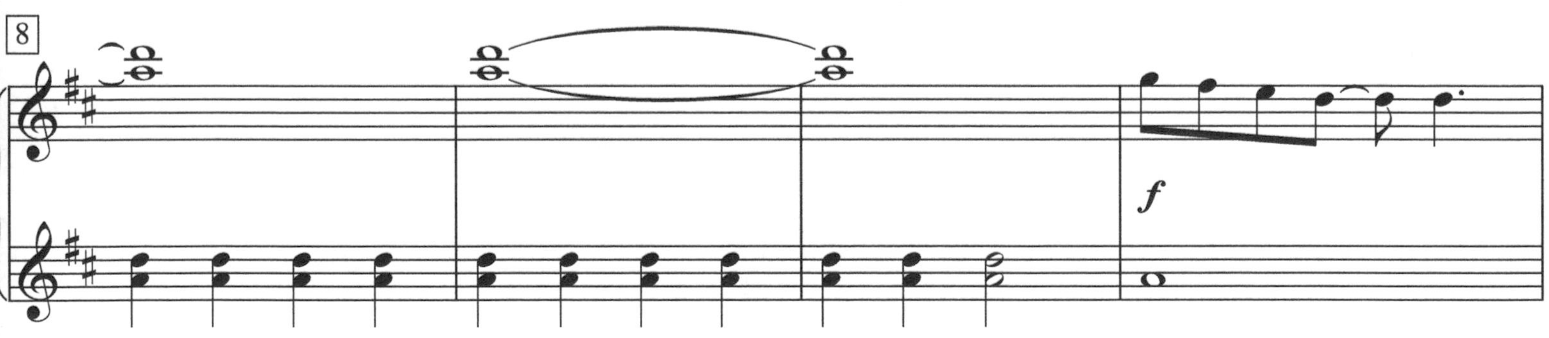

16
mf

20
cresc.

24
To Coda
1.
2.

28
Play 3 times
f
cresc.

PRIMO

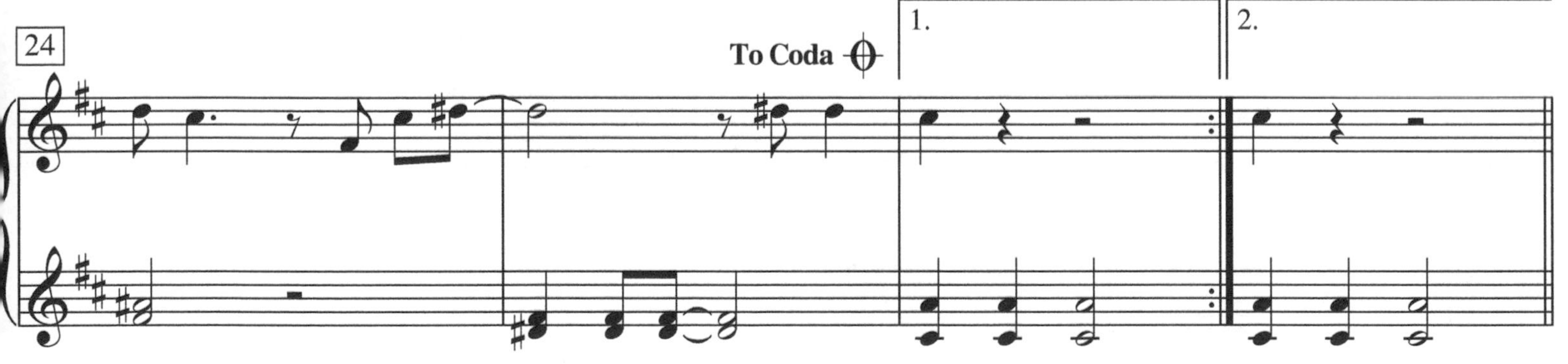

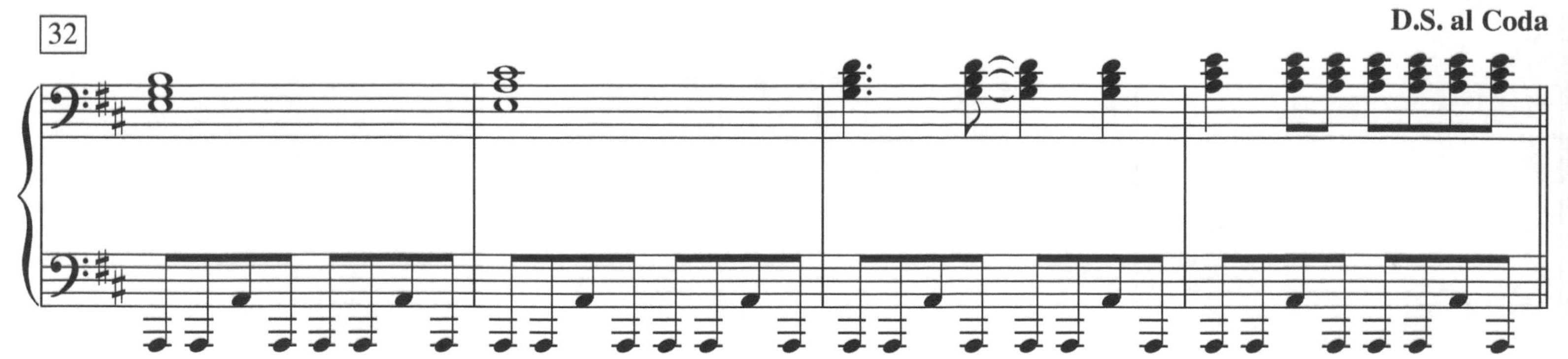
32
D.S. al Coda

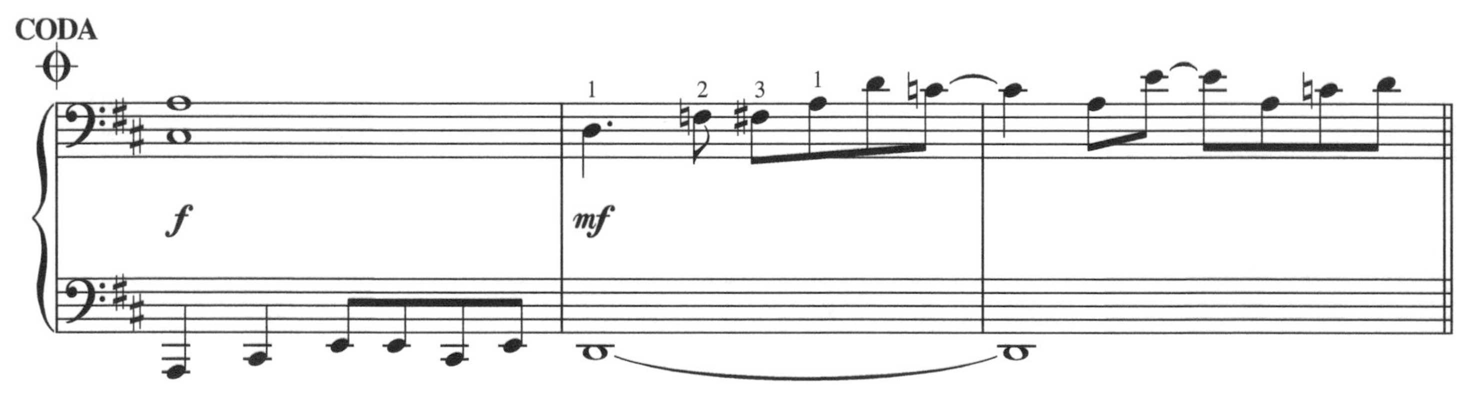
CODA
1
2
3
1
f
mf

39
Play 3 times
f

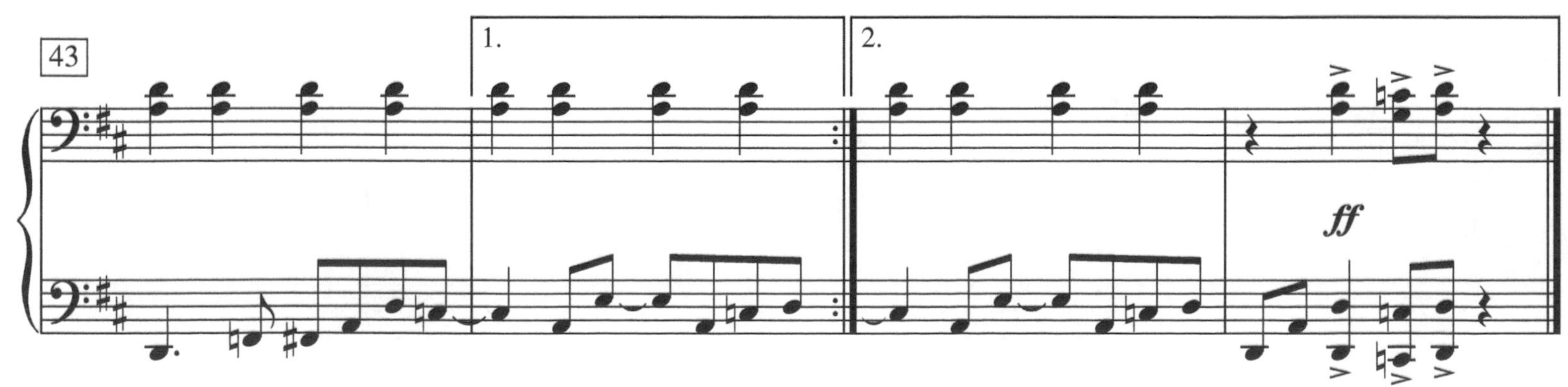
43
1.
2.
ff

PRIMO

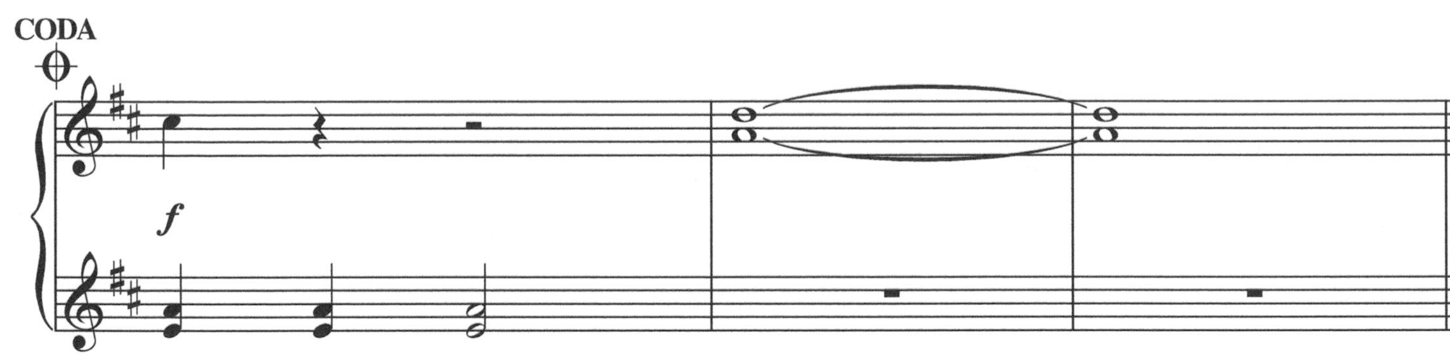

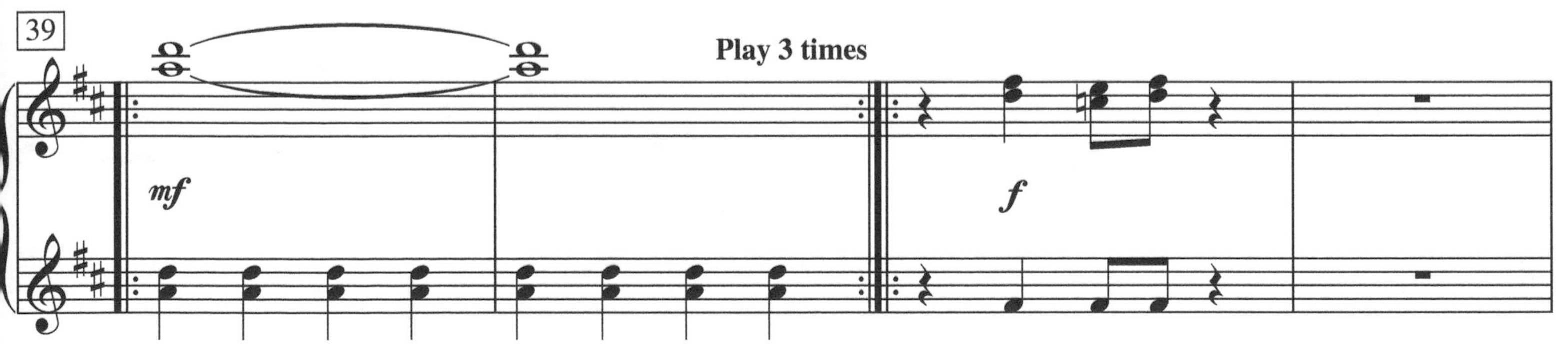

THE FOOL ON THE HILL

SECONDO

Words and Music by JOHN LENNON
and PAUL McCARTNEY

Relaxed, with a lilt

THE FOOL ON THE HILL

PRIMO

Words and Music by JOHN LENNON
and PAUL McCARTNEY

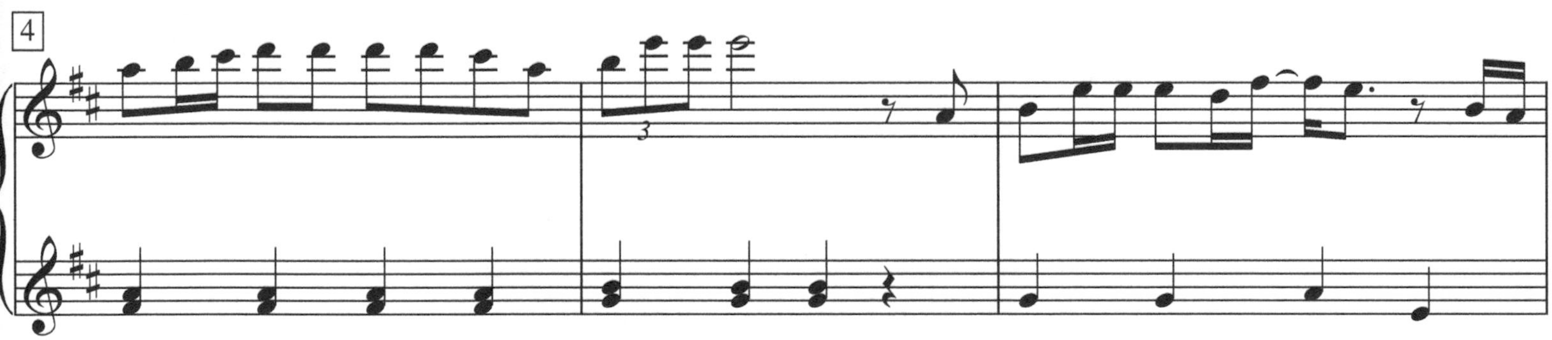

SECONDO

14
mf
17
20
mp
22
24
rit. e dim.
p

HERE, THERE AND EVERYWHERE

SECONDO

Words and Music by JOHN LENNON
and PAUL McCARTNEY

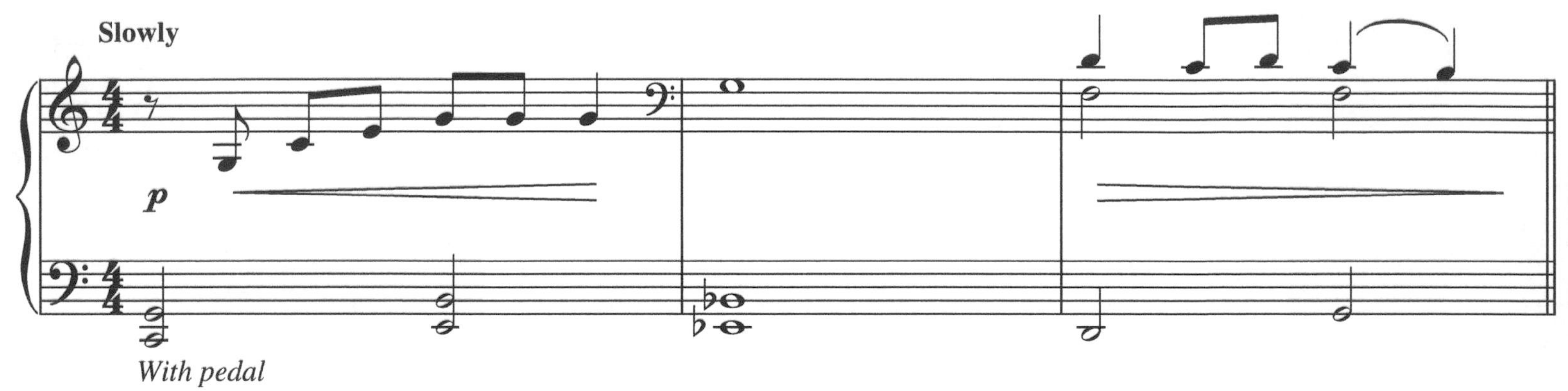

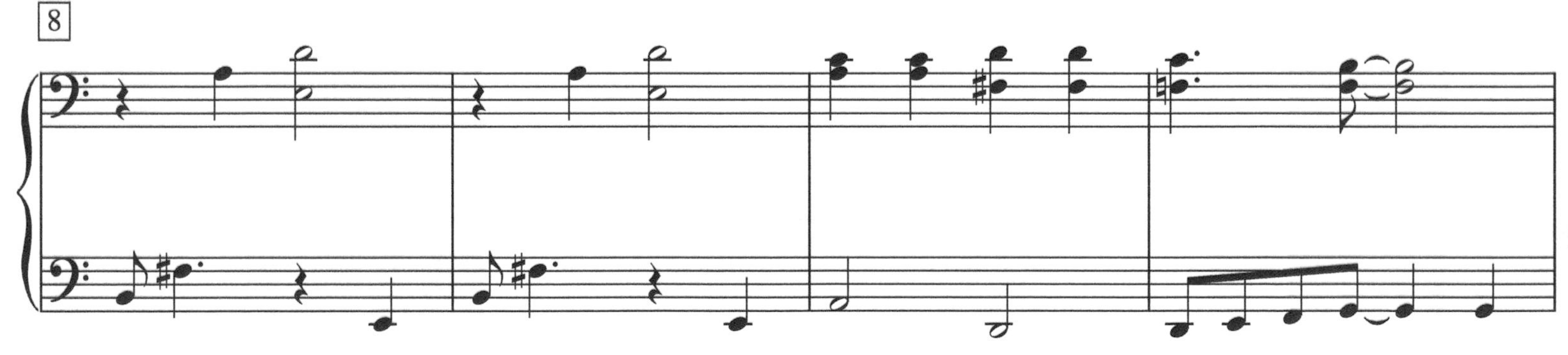

HERE, THERE AND EVERYWHERE

PRIMO

Words and Music by JOHN LENNON
and PAUL McCARTNEY

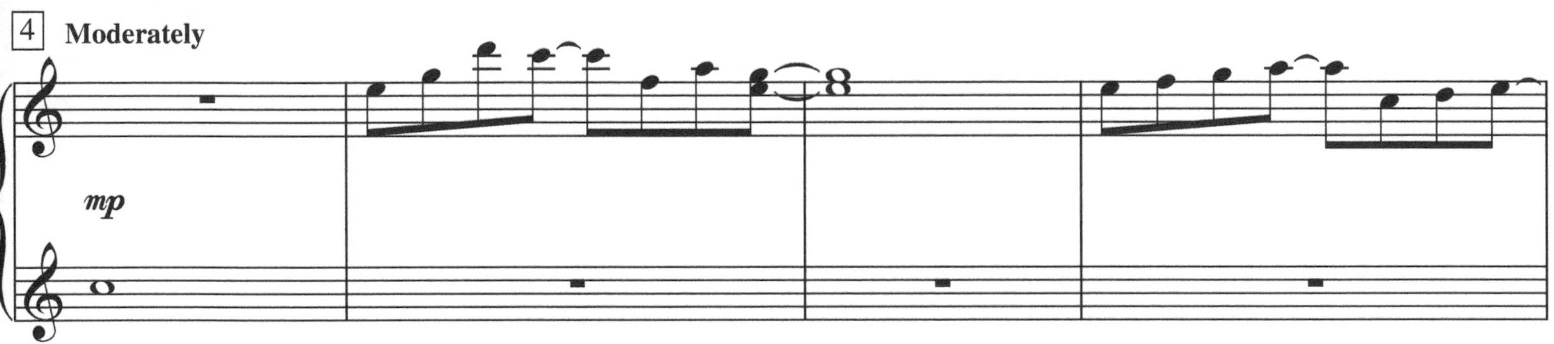

SECONDO

16

20
p

24
mp

28

SECONDO

32

36
mf

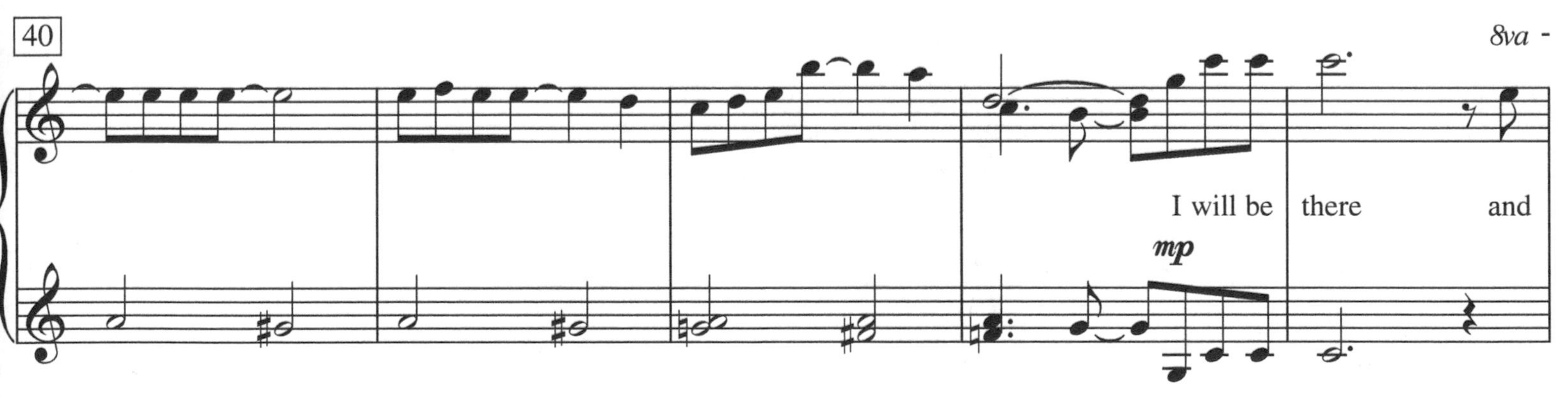
40
8va
I will be
there
and
mp

45
(8va)
ev - 'ry - where,
here,
there
and
ev - 'ry - where.
rit.
pp

HEY JUDE

SECONDO

Words and Music by JOHN LENNON
and PAUL McCARTNEY

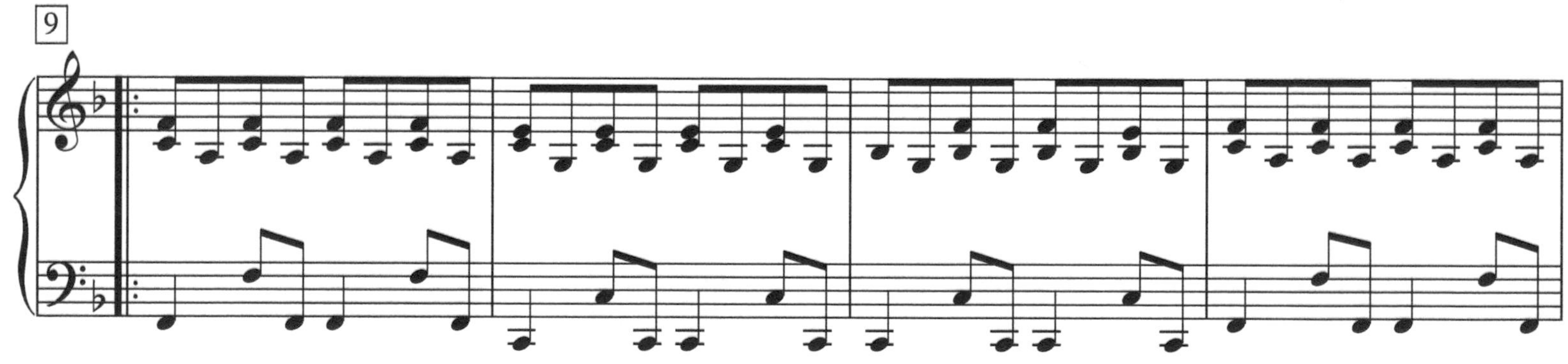

HEY JUDE

PRIMO

Words and Music by JOHN LENNON
and PAUL McCARTNEY

Moderately

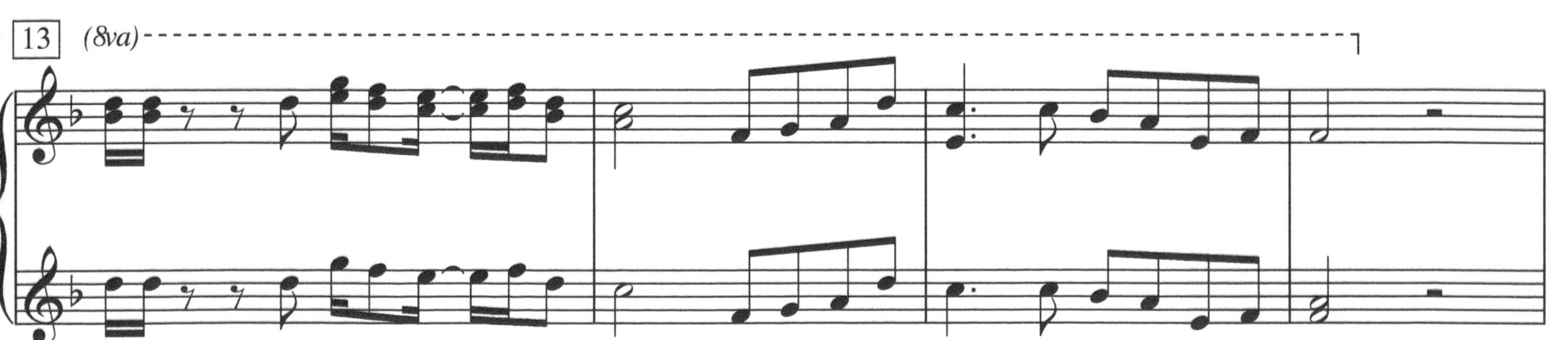

17

21

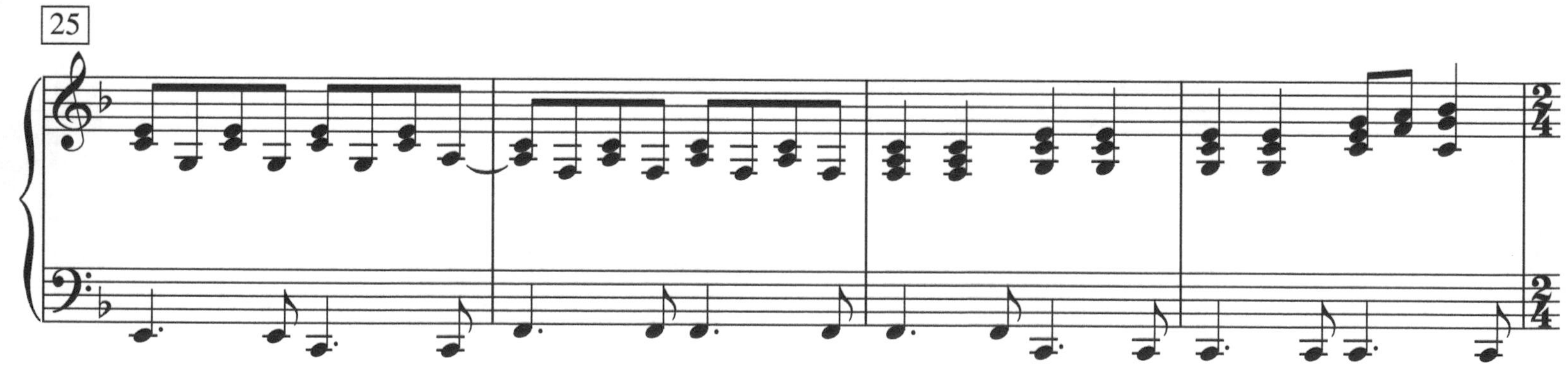
25

29
1.
2.

PRIMO

33

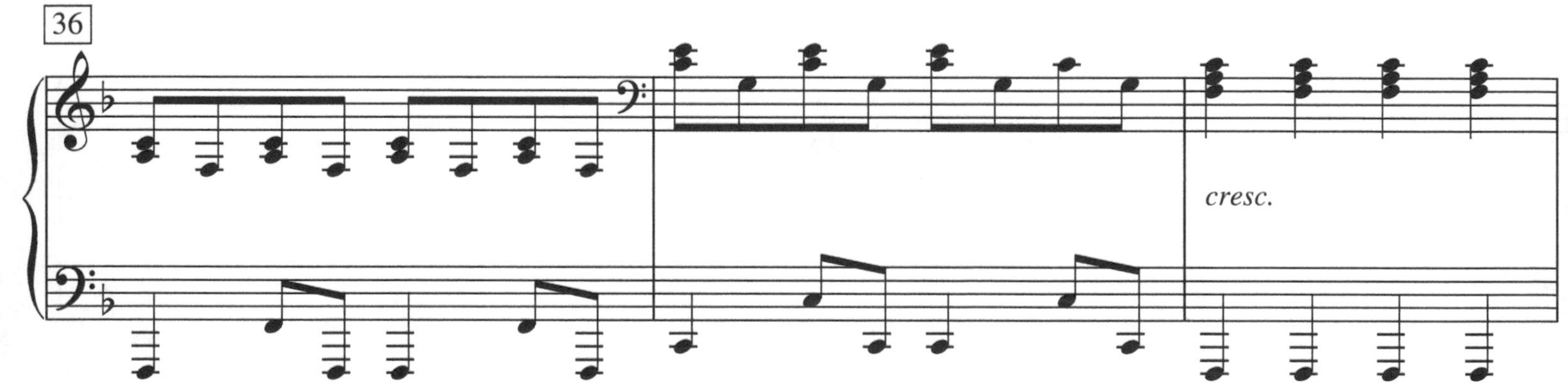
36
cresc.

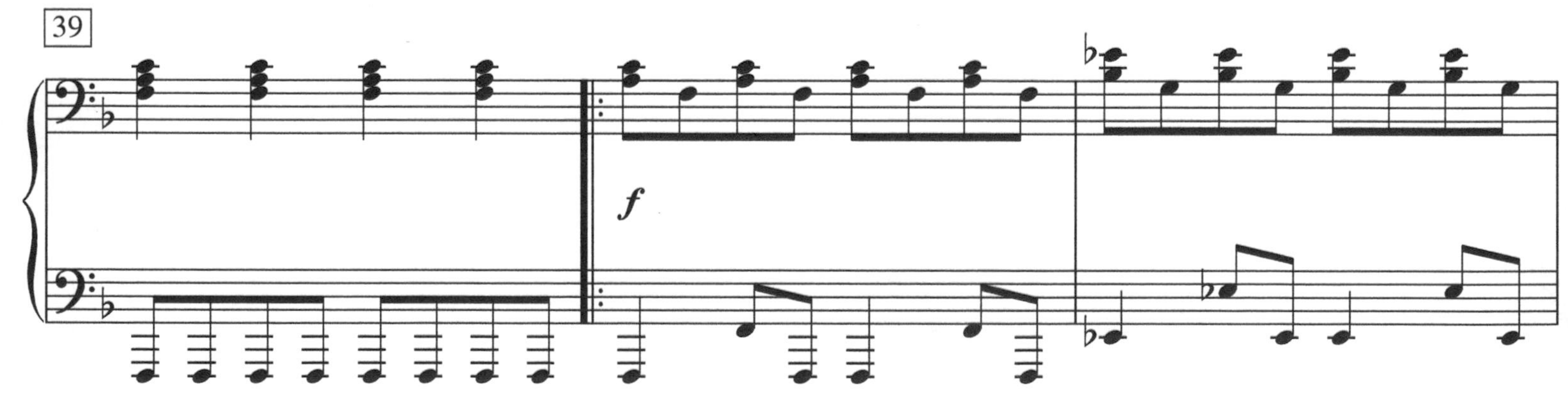
39
f

42
Play 4 times, ad lib.

33
(8va)
1

36
(8va)
cresc.

39
Da da da
da da da da,
f

42
Play 4 times, ad lib.
Da da da da, hey
Jude.

THE LONG AND WINDING ROAD

SECONDO

Words and Music by JOHN LENNON
and PAUL McCARTNEY

THE LONG AND WINDING ROAD

PRIMO

Words and Music by JOHN LENNON
and PAUL McCARTNEY

13
2.
mf

16
mp

19
cresc.

22

PRIMO

25
mf

28
To Coda
mp

31
D.S. al Coda
cresc.

CODA

25
f

28
To Coda
mp

31
D.S. al Coda
cresc.
mf

CODA

MICHELLE

SECONDO

Words and Music by JOHN LENNON
and PAUL McCARTNEY

MICHELLE

PRIMO

Words and Music by JOHN LENNON
and PAUL McCARTNEY

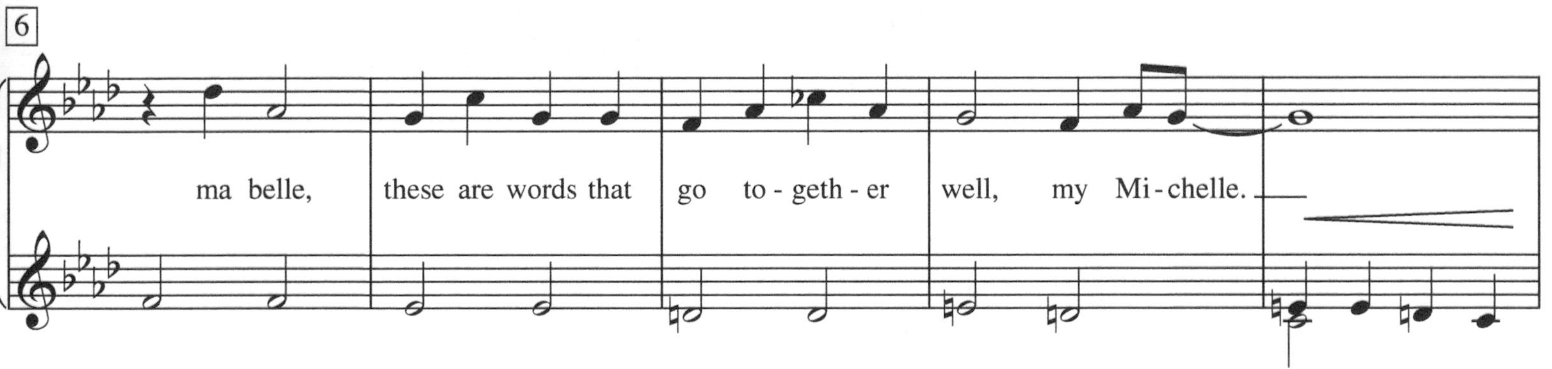

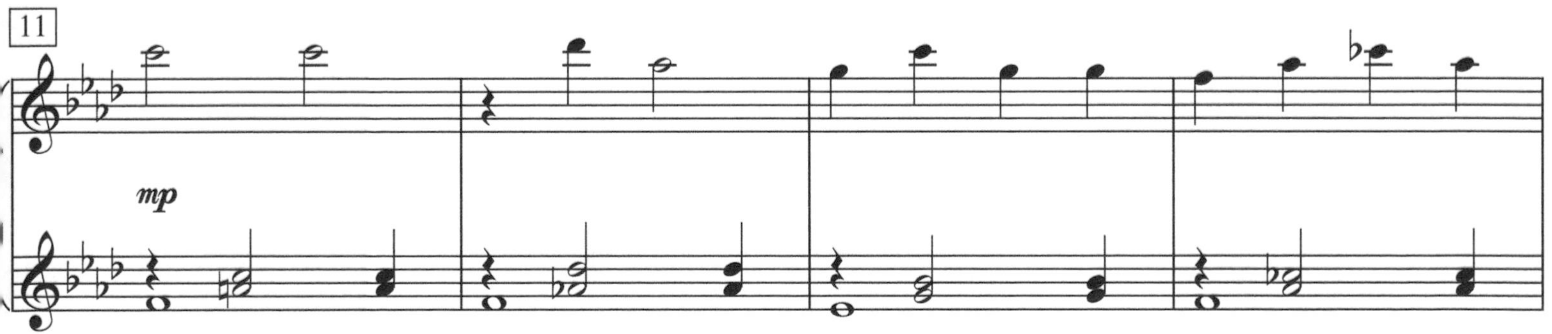

19
23
p
26
mf
1
3-1
3
3
3
30
3
3
3
3
mf
34

19
23
mp
26
mp
30
3
3
3
f
34

38
p
43
mf
3
48
p
53
1
3-1
mf
3
3
3
3
57
3
f molto rall.
p

38
mp
43
p
4 2
48
mp
53
57
3
f molto rall.
p

WHEN I'M SIXTY-FOUR

SECONDO

Words and Music by JOHN LENNON
and PAUL McCARTNEY

WHEN I'M SIXTY-FOUR

PRIMO

Words and Music by JOHN LENNON
and PAUL McCARTNEY

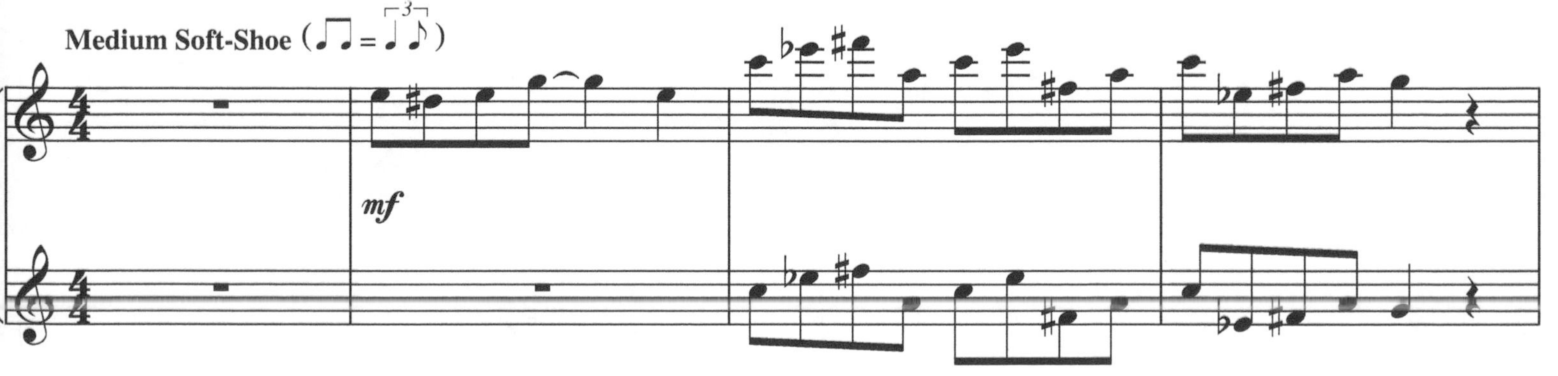

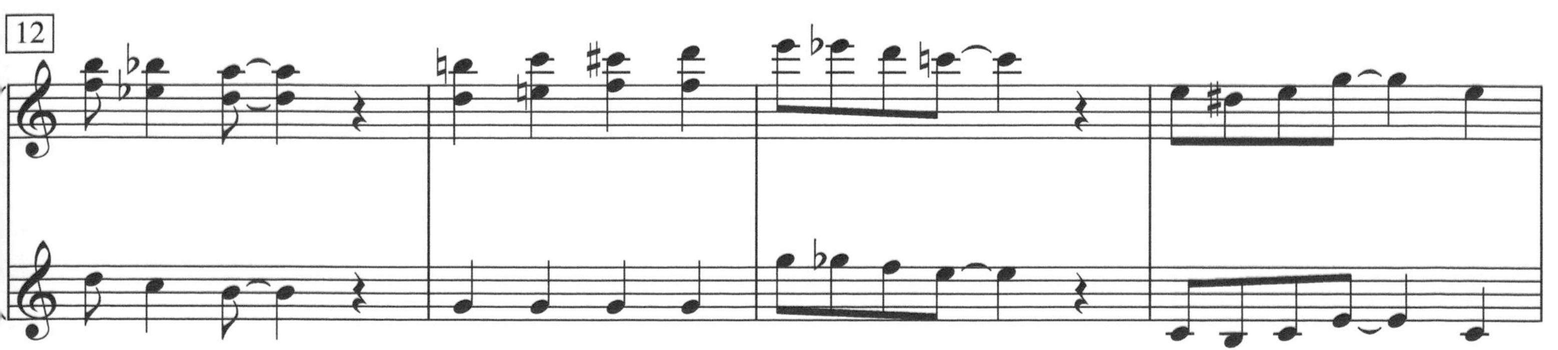

16
20
f
24
p
29
mp
p
34

16
20
24
29
34

38
f
42
46
mp
50
54
To Coda
p

38
mp
42
46
mf
50
54
To Coda
mf

58
mp
63
p
68
72
D.S. al Coda
CODA
mf
76
f

58
63
68
72
D.S. al Coda
CODA
76
mf
f

YESTERDAY

SECONDO

Words and Music by JOHN LENNON
and PAUL McCARTNEY

YESTERDAY

PRIMO

Words and Music by JOHN LENNON
and PAUL McCARTNEY

17
1
2

21
3
mp

25
5

29

17
3

21
p

25
3

29
mf

33

37
p

41
4
2
1

45
rit.

33
3

37
Yes - ter - day,
mf
2
1
1

41
love was such an eas - y
game to play.
Now I need a place to
hide a - way, oh
4
3
5
3
5
2

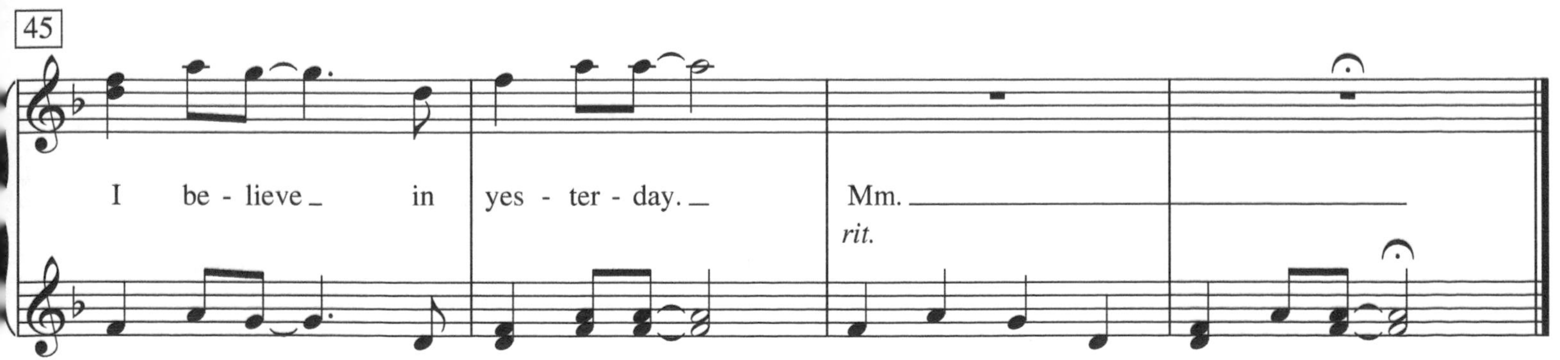
45
I be - lieve in
yes - ter - day.
Mm.
rit.

PIANO DUETS

PIANO DUET PLAY-ALONG

The **Piano Duet Play-Along** series is an excellent source for 1 piano, 4 hand duets in every genre! It also gives you the flexibility to rehearse or perform piano duets anytime, anywhere! Play these delightful tunes with a partner, or use the accompanying audio to play along with either the Secondo or Primo part on your own. The audio files are enhanced so performers can adjust the recording to any tempo without changing pitch.

1. Piano Favorites
00290546 Book/CD Pack $14.95

2. Movie Favorites
00290547 Book/CD Pack $14.95

3. Broadway for Two
00290548 Book/CD Pack $14.95

4. The Music of Andrew Lloyd Webber™
00290549 Book/CD Pack $14.95

5. Disney Favorites
00290550 Book/CD Pack $14.95

6. Disney Songs
00290551 Book/CD Pack $14.95

7. Classical Music
00290552 Book/CD Pack $14.95

8. Christmas Classics
00290554 Book/CD Pack $14.95

9. Hymns
00290556 Book/CD Pack $14.95

10. The Sound of Music
00290557 Book/CD Pack $17.99

11. Disney Early Favorites
00290558 Book/CD Pack $16.95

12. Disney Movie Songs
00290559 Book/Online Audio $16.99

13. Movie Hits
00290560 Book/CD Pack $14.95

14. Les Misérables
00290561 Book/CD Pack $16.95

15. God Bless America® & Other Songs for a Better Nation
00290562 Book/CD Pack $14.99

16. Disney Classics
00290563 Book/CD Pack $16.95

19. Pirates of the Caribbean
00290566 Book/CD Pack $16.95

20. Wicked
00290567 Book/CD Pack $16.99

21. Peanuts®
00290568 Book/CD Pack $16.99

22. Rodgers & Hammerstein
00290569 Book/CD Pack $14.99

23. Cole Porter
00290570 Book/CD Pack $14.99

24. Christmas Carols
00290571 Book/CD Pack $14.95

25. Wedding Songs
00290572 Book/CD Pack $14.99

26. Love Songs
00290573 Book/CD Pack $14.99

27. Romantic Favorites
00290574 Book/CD Pack $14.99

28. Classical for Two
00290575 Book/CD Pack $14.99

29. Broadway Classics
00290576 Book/CD Pack $14.99

30. Jazz Standards
00290577 Book/CD Pack $14.99

31. Pride and Prejudice
00290578 Book/CD Pack $14.99

32. Sondheim for Two
00290579 Book/CD Pack $16.99

33. Twilight
00290580 Book/CD Pack $14.99

36. Holiday Favorites
00290583 Book/CD Pack $14.99

37. Christmas for Two
00290584 Book/CD Pack $14.99

38. Lennon & McCartney Favorites
00290585 Book/CD Pack $14.99

39. Lennon & McCartney Hits
00290586 Book/CD Pack $14.99

40. Classical Themes
00290588 Book/Online Audio $14.99

41. The Phantom of the Opera
00290589 Book/CD Pack $16.99

42. Glee
00290590 Book/CD Pack $16.99

43. A Merry Little Christmas
00102044 Book/CD Pack $14.99

44. Frozen
00128260 Book/Online Audio $14.99

45. Coldplay
00141054 Book/Online Audio $14.99

View complete songlists at
Hal Leonard Online at **www.halleonard.com**